Small Business Lead Generation & Cold Email B2B & B2C

SADANAND PUJARI

Published by SADANAND PUJARI, 2023.

Table of Contents

Copyright

Copyright © 2023 by **SADANAND PUJARI**

Small Business Lead Generation & Cold Email B2B & B2C

First Edition: Nov 2023

Book Design by **SADANAND PUJARI**

About

If you want to make any idea a successful one, you're going to need some outside help. Whether it's finding customers or just expanding your contact list, cold emails are the way to go. In this easy-to-follow Book, we're going to focus on building a lead generation campaign that will grow your business, your network, and your opportunities.

Cold email may have built up a bit of a bad reputation, but that's only because people don't know how to do it well. When used properly, the technique opens up access to any individual in the world, whether that's the average shopper or a Fortune 500 CEO.

Need investors or clients for your business? Use cold email. Need interviews for your podcast? Use cold email. Simply want to meet someone you find fascinating? Use cold email.

You may run a small retail business or work on the sales team at a startup. You may just want to gauge interest in a business idea you've conjured up. Whatever it is you're trying to do, the chapters in this Book will teach you how to reach out to people and capture their attention instantly.

We'll take you through the entire cold email process from figuring out your target audience and building a hit list to effective copywriting and follow-up techniques. Campaigns can be a rollercoaster, so we'll also show you what to do when things aren't going your way. Plus, you'll learn the best software to use and how to automate the most time-consuming parts — even if you have no budget at all.

This Book focuses equally on B2B and B2C sales with techniques and customizations for both scenarios. So whether you want to rake in those customers or secure a million dollar deal, you'll walk away with a strategy that works for you. All you need to start is an email account.

Introduction

If you have an online business, you're selling something, it might be a product of your own, a service you provide an affiliate product or most likely multiple affiliate products, whatever it is you're selling, you need to leave. In fact, in most of the major industries, the average cost of a single leave is 20 or more. That's valuable.

But you will have to pay that kind of money because you are about to learn exactly how to position yourself so you can easily come back with an unlimited amount of a high quality lease without breaking the bank. So what exactly is a lead? A lead is a potential buyer and then more importantly, a qualified prospect that has been proven to be interested in your products or services.

Potential customers or client elites are not guaranteed to buy, but they are far more likely to because they are shown interest in your niche market. How does one go about generating and quantifying the lease you need to entice them to offer their contact information in exchange for something valuable in Miami? Be free.

Report a training with a discount or coupon or something else, but it should be something they will be interested in only if they will also likely be interested in whatever you're selling. In other words, offering a discount coupon for a coffee shop is not going to get you qualified. The lease if you're selling model cars, a guide on how to lose weight is now going to get you qualified for the lease if you're offering a graphic design service.

Sure, a few of those people might be interested in what you're selling, but you want people who have a clearly demonstrated level of interest in the types of product or service you're offering. Here's a simple example. If you're offering a dog walking service, you might offer a free report on training your dog or how to get a bargain patta supplies or even a coupon for 50 percent off the customer's first working session to begin forming elements to generate leads.

Number one, you need a system. Number two, you need to have a lead magnet. Number three, you need a script. Page number four, you need traffic. We're going to devote a whole chapter to each of these four elements so you will learn more about how

to start generating leads as you move through these Books. By the end of this Book, you will be able to get ready to start connecting with Ray Hosp Perspex in your niche market so you can instantly maximize your income and expand your outreach. So let's get started.

Step One: The System

The first thing you absolutely must do if you want to, generally a staff or service member allows you to do the database of Aleah through a Web form. Most people simply use that autoresponder service, such as chimp male or light a Weber or get a response. But there are also services that collect, store, manage and search men, different types of information.

If you need more details from your lease, if all you need is to collect its name and the email, which is fine for most online marketing purposes, you can just use a single autoresponder system. Here's a list of some of the most popular autoresponder services. Each of these services is widely respected and most have similar features and pricing.

If you're just getting started, email chain and the Miller Lite have free words and you can use them for a while. Machismo later elaborate and get a response, if you're looking to collect more in-depth information, you might want to go with CRM or customer relationship management software. This type of software has in-depth information collection and the management allows you to be the database of customer information that you can use for marketing purposes.

A simple example is agile CRM agent CRM is one of the most popular and powerful CRM systems out there and you can start with a free account to give you a try. You can have up to 10 users with a trial. You don't have to enter any credit card information to get started. Agel will let you set up an autoresponder cup in from a B split passing segment your releases and then even predict customer behavior in the future.

Best of all, Agile CRM has some of the best pricing in the industry. These plans start at just eight point nine dollars per month after the trial. Infusionsoft is one of the most well-known CRM systems, Aldar. They have a hugely powerful suite of features, including cinching with over two hundred other services from Gmail to big ecommerce, Shopify to Commerce. Infusionsoft has extremely powerful analytics, a full fledged sales pipeline button and much more.

The biggest drawbacks to Infusionsoft is pricing, which starts as a not one ninety nine and the skills aboard its more powerful software. But the price may be a bit high if you're just getting started. Still, Spurs is another well known CRM. They have a huge arsenal of tools available, including they have plans starting at just twenty five per month for the generation alone. So they are affordable for smaller companies who won't have a lot of users.

The setting of the software if you don't need the other wants the features. You can make the cheapest plan just for generating these. They need a management system, letting you keep track of all the stages of customer interaction and transactions and. The agent is very affordable CRM system that has a wealth of features, including email tracking all about Albon along the call, tracking sales activity, tracking real time alerts and updates, mass email sent calendars thinking and more plans start at just one night per month, making a great option for new companies and those who are not doing enough business to support a price of one of the more expensive options. Ones are decided which system you're going to use and then your son off one account. And to familiarize yourself with how it works is time to move on to the next step.

Step Two: The Offer

Once you have chosen your system and the set of your initial campaign, it's time to think about creating your offer, which many people refer to as your leading segment is kind of like a fishing where you release the fish in your leg and Megamind is a bather that draws them in.

Remember, this offer should help you directly to your chosen demographic. You can't expect to catch a catfish with a fish flush. You mean for big bucks? What is possible is not likely in your stand a much better chance of catching a catfish with something that's known to appeal, such as a chicken livers or earthworms or a stink bait. Just trying to think about what might appeal to your target audience.

What would they be interested in learning? They don't already know. What would they be interested in getting a discount on? Most people create a special report as their lead measurement is usually 10 to 20 pages, but maybe up to 50 or so, depending on how much you want to say. Longer reports are more appropriate when you have a complex subject, and I'm not selling information on the topic with them, or if are you in really a state of selling houses, you can give away a 50 page guide on how to find the perfect house, including information about stuff like zoning regulations, homeowners associations, utilities, the front page and frontage and the home inspection. But if you're selling a Horse Book, I see a shorter report saying plenty of pages on a small segment of the topic will be much more pertinent because you don't want to give away all your information for free.

You can always ulcer the lead of megamix or purchase a high quality product that you can use. This will save you a lot of time. If you're into Internet marketing or B2B business to business field, you might be interested in signing off with automated at least a profits monthly program which delivers fully automated generation packages per month and includes a report Askwith, Page and Syncopate.

All you have to do is the pace of your shopping code and upload everything. You might also consider just offering a half a discount on a coupon to lease, especially if you have

a product that is in demand in your speech. This is especially useful if you have a recurring business model or a sales funnel with up sales that will allow you to use the initial sale as a loss leader and make more money on the back end later. Once you have your lead ready before they add a link to it and your autoresponder service as a follow up of their people up in, you don't want to have to send all those freebies out manually.

Check out Autoresponder How files to find out how to set up a follow up email that contains a link to your leader. Magonet The process might be slightly different for each service, but it's not difficult. It's about as easy as sending an email. Then it's time to create a script page to promote it.

Step Three: The Squeeze Page

Your script page is your lead generation page. This is a Web page created specifically to collect information from people. And then once they do, you, Autoresponder will direct them to the page where they can download their freebie. These pages should be relatively short. It's not like a long sales letter.

People don't need that much convincing when something is free, when they do need some. After all, they don't want to give out their personal contact details unless they really think your leading measurement will benefit them for this reason is to have just enough information to entice the reader into taking action. If it's too long, people will get bored. And even before that.

Generally speaking, a script page should consist of highflying. This needs to immediately capture their attention and persuade them to continue reading Subhi online. This requires a little more information and a worse as your high line supporting Agent Pooty points quake that just about highlights how your perspective benefits. By subscribing to your newsletter or entering your funnel call to action direct a prompt.

I instruct your prospect how to complete the process of signing up for your free offer. You need a generation form usually generated by your autoresponder service, only the generation service with wearer's form fields and above and to submit it information. QuickTrip, eliminate your workload if you kasser up to a service that provides monthly lead generation packages that include script pages, high quality content, and you can send out to your list and everything else you need to start collecting leaves and booting your back in the system.

This service is called automated, at least a process, and it was designed to eliminate the workload involved in building a lead generation system by providing you with everything you need to get started. You should check out the proper model stock home for the automated Lisa Prophase information to collect. Most people collect only the names and email addresses of their lives, but you might need more information than that depending on your niche market and whether you wish to further our segment, your list and identify potential customers through demographic based data.

This name and address of potential customers is proper enough information for general marketing purposes. But what if you are selling a high end product or service like real estate or legal service or something? Require one on one contact, like coaching. You will want to begin collecting as much information as possible to help you better and then come back with their potential customers.

In cases like this it is probably a better idea to ask for name, address, telephone number and email. You might even need additional information such as data brokers. If you are selling something adult only, for example, or you get more detailed information such as a breed of dog they own or their income. You don't want to ask for too much information. Was it just cause people to get frustrated and leave without fulfilling your form, but you want to get just enough information to make sure they are qualified?

In other words, what information do you really need to know up front and what can you get there later in the selling process? Once your scritch page is set up in your ADDAE, the legal maximum to your autoresponder service is time to start sending traffic to your squeeze page.

Step Four: Traffic

The three previous steps were pretty easy, even if you are only to make them from scratch, and then you need time to learn how to use your autoresponder or CRM, you can complete the other three steps in a few days. And most you might think of traffic is the hardest part, but it's actually a lot simpler than you think to get traffic.

We're going to take a look at a few of the best strategies for getting the traffic free and freeze traffic. As far as free traffic goes, there's only one measure that's quick enough to generate traffic. Starting today, I didn't have a happy learning curve and poor calling to traffic, tech and convert social media. Keep in mind that certain markets are more inclined to use certain social networks than others. So it's important to look at your market and be certain you are focusing most of your time and energy on those locations.

While you can still use other social networks, most of your efforts should be focused on those sites that have a higher concentration of your targeted demographic. We're going to look at a few of the most popular social networks and how you can locate your target demographic, each one in order to find out which one you should concentrate on. Facebook locating your target demographic on Facebook is relatively easy to begin by searching for a topic related to our niche and the front pages and groups that feature a niche.

For example, if you're offering the dog walking service, you want to search for things like groups for pet owners in your city or State Farm. How many people are in those groups and how many groups there are? This will give you a rough idea of how many people you can Alridge reach in Facebook dromedaries groups and then participate in making sure you follow her rules. If you don't allow promotions, you won't need to contact the group administrators and ask for permission to other the ties your service on the right. You should be able to pipe in.

If people have to ask about dog walking services, you can also start your own group, which is your best option. This will give you a source of traffic that turns into leaves any time. You should also start a Facebook page for your business and you can even include a link to your script page on your Facebook page. Pinterest. Pinterest is a lot like another online board. You can have multiple boards and an email just with links, sort of like a bookmark pool marking a page.

You can find out how popular your niche is on Pinterest by performing a search and then clicking the worst to find out how many people have Borza related to your niche and how many followers those boards have. You should also search Pince for the niche and to see how many recipients each one has. These will let you know how interested the people are.

Pinterest has a huge amount of traffic and this is relatively easy to assess just by following accounts that have some connection to your niche and opening content related to your niche and then using keywords in your board names and description, you don't need to have some interesting content. So it's a good idea to have a blog or a Website that you use to post content related to your files. For example, you could have a thought care blog for your dog walking service and post useful information for pet owners.

One important thing to note is that Pinterest is Habila inmate based. So if you are in need of good images to pin that relate to your article with them, if you're posting an article called a Five Tips for Housebreaking Your Puppy, you won't want to include a photo of a dog being trained or something related to housebreaking puppy and have the title of your article on that image.

If you take a look at the Pinterest, you will see that most images are taller than they are wide because they're Taika, the most screen real estate since they are constrained by wells, by waste. But how much more space to expend less land chapters? Just try to make sure your image follows the same format. Instagram is premise, a redeployment for video content, and then you can get a lot of traffic from it, especially if your business is related to fashion, beauty, art, lifestyle, food and the cooking, crafts and other topics that are popular.

You can get a good indication of what's popular on the ground by opening the app and clicking. The search icon searches for a term related to your name, friends and clicking text. This will allow you to show you how many posts are currently on the site. You do that phase and as well as lots of related phrases. Muzammil Weissert photogs. I see millions of posts with such hashtag-like tags.

Talks of Instagram ducks or ducks, ducks tag around or a Duck City, you can also click the people tab and create some of the top four files to see how many followers they have. This is not a good indicator of interest in your topic. There are three important steps to get traffic and funnel your profile, fill out your profile and include a link to your Web site or scrutinizer.

Make sure that you have an interesting photo, either yourself or something related to your niche with your profile page and include a link because you can't include the links in the descriptions of your individual policies. Just tell people to check your profile for link posts. Often Instagram poses scroll by and go quickly if someone is following a lot of profiles. So the best way to get seen is to post as often as possible.

Don't spend just a few posts a day is fine, but spread them out every few hours. And don't forget at least five relevant hashtags. Every poll follows people who are related to you and many will follow you and others will find out. Follow your old people's profile. It's a good idea to follow at least 20 new accounts each day, which you can find easily through the search function. And the referrals from other people stick mostly to following accounts related to your niche because you want to be qualified, at least not just a high follower account. Other social networks.

There are other social networks that can be effective too, depending on your market. I suggest giving each of them a try to see how they can do for your particular market, but you might want to concentrate on your effort. On the other side, we talked about earlier in this chapter, pay to traffic. I don't recommend using paper traffic as in you or so a good amount of free traffic at your speech page photo and tassi the conversion rate.

If you are not getting Minnelli's, you might want to make some tweaks to your script page and the lead among men to increase those convergence. Once you are happy with how your page is converting, you can start sending some pay to traffic to it. Let's look at some of the most effective paid ad platforms. Those are generally the most profitable, but they may not work on the edges equally.

So be sure to check your word and carefully tweak as needed and the KUNR that are not performing Facebook ads. Facebook is generally considered one of the best advertising platforms because the ads are typically affordable and this is mainly because of how well they are able to target ads to the appropriate parties. Remember, when you talk about how important it is to get qualified, that is Facebook is Brenin for that, because they have an incredible they are the ones that are targeting options.

You can target the people based on age, gender, location, marital status, just about anything you can think of. Plus you can target your interest, shopping habits. And there's so much more sticking, bizarre example of using a local dog walking business. You can talk to people in your city or surrounding cities and who are dog owners. You can seriously get that specific. You and your ad pay attention to the table and you're creating the regular news feed and the mobile news feed format are considered the most profitable.

Keep in mind that the price you pay for your ad on Facebook is heavily based on your CAR, which is great and it's important to design the most effective and possible. If you notice an ad has a lousy PR post the ad and make the changes. Keep tweaking until you find the right combination to bring in qualified, at least at a low cost. Facebook has a great guide to help you get started. Being asked Beanz at PayPal isn't nearly as competitive as many others because they have much less traffic in Google, Facebook or in some other platforms.

However, you can still get a lot of traffic at the very low price because a lower competition means that you can actually get more traffic than you at a more competitive size because in many instances you could be the only advertiser in general being a PPC platform, just like a Google ad network. So if you're already familiar with AdWords, you shouldn't have too much trouble being trained if you're not familiar with the platform.

Other ad platforms, there are platforms that you can explore as well, such as YouTube, Pinterest, Twitter, Instagram, Google AdWords and many others. But these can be a little tricky to master. The other three platforms we discussed, there is a more expensive, more competitive or harder to master for. This reason I suggest exploring other platforms once a year, Mussert, the other three we discussed and are getting consistent results.

Extra Strategies

There are a few things you can do to take your lead generation to the next level. In this chapter, we're going to look at a few of those big splashes. The big welcome splash is a fantastic way to really grab a visitor's attention the moment you arrive at your website and get them to pop in. See, wizards have become immune to pop ups and they get really annoyed with all of the sneaky tactics, like an expert in their tiny and a collared, almost like a bigram and a recording of him before they can even read your content. They don't respond to these as well as they used to.

They just leave the beat of what a big welcome is a plug-in for WordPress that will eliminate a lot of this winter's frustration while still letting you attract attention and grab those leads. You can create as many welcome messages as you need to, including a different splash screen for each page on your site, if you like. Sinestro says SREP is another powerful WordPress plugin.

Never let you create a cool chapter in as that can include the lead generation form. These are much more interesting and attention grabbing than Papas or Stender on page forms. Save Stripe is great when you use it in conjunction with Big Up because you have two chances to capture the lead and the people can respond differently to different offers. Retargeting retargeting is these truly powerful advertising methods that can be used at many different out of platforms such as Facebook.

This is one of the techniques because isn't it particularly difficult to set up retargeting that allows you to specifically target the people you have already reached in order to pull them back in and get a second chance at converting them? It's also useful because it allows you to target your existing leads into sales. You will need to set up a retargeting pixel on your script page.

Whichever platform you're using will give you the code you need to add to your page. This will trigger visitors' behavior and target them again later. You can learn more about the targeting on Facebook at.

System From Start To Finish

In this Book, you have to learn how to set up your own powerful lead, the generation system from start to finish, whether you're just looking to collect email addresses to brutalize so you can make philia offers or your won't products or you need more detailed information for big ticket items. You're not armed with exactly what you need to start collecting those leaves.

Remember, it's a widow to collect qualifications. You get to have a list of amenities, but it won't do you any good unless those people are interested in what you have to offer. It is much better to have solid and qualified leads than it is to have a meaning. Unqualified, unqualifiedly, unless, of course, you're selling something that has an extremely wide area of interest. Start by choosing the right leader generation service for you. Most of them have trials so you can test them all to see which one works best for your needs and then which one you find easier to you next age or lead a management.

And this offer should be something related to your niche or something that your target market will likely be interested in once your lead in Megamind is already. Your Squeeze page. Remember to keep these pages simple and focus on letting people know exactly what they will get and then why it will benefit them when they sign up.

Finally, send some traffic to your squit page. Starboy is a free traffic refund to your page to get a good account. We're going to rate and to send the paired traffic once and you know your page is converting. Well, is that simple? Now like this, get out there and start generating all of these you need for your business. Good. And down here, I will see you in my next Book.

Resources

MailChimp

>> http://www.mailchimp.com

MailerLite

>> http://www.MailerLite.com[1]

AWeber

>> http://www.aweber.com

GetResponse

>> http://www.GetResponse.com[2]

CRM Systems

Agile CRM

>> https://www.agilecrm.com/marketing-automation-software

Infusionsoft

>> http://www.infusionsoft.com

Salesforce

>> http://www.salesforce.com

FreeAgent

---

1. http://www.mailerlite.com

2. http://www.getresponse.com

>> http://www.freeagentcrm.com

Lead Generation

Well, and congratulations on finishing the lead generation Book in this bonus. I want to show you how I started up my own lead generation fondles and to show you how it works. First of all, I want to highlight why we wanted to be the generation. Right. If you have any experience in business or investing right, you can see the difference right away.

If you are working on the investment, you only want to make the right decision at the right time. Right. That means that you have some money. You want a lot of money to make money for you. So you don't have to deal with other people. You don't have to even need any connection with people to make money because the exchange is right there. Right.

When you go to the stock exchange, you can buy some products, buy some stocks from that and have some money, as your head of Crosio brokerage works harder for some fees. Right. But it's so easy to start a buy and sell product, sell stocks and to, you know, possibly make some money from the 20s with investing. You want to make the right decision instead of making more connections to sell people.

So you are literally on the buy business for investing. But on the other side, if you run a business, no matter if you are selling a product or service, it is all about selling. Right. So because you are literally offering one solution to a problem of other people, it will be individual people that will be called in to see right to consumers and you with some business, some small business, who is just starting all who want to make some more money. Right. That's to talk about the right to business and in any other way, you try to help those people.

You know, if they have some problems, you want to solve their problems. You want to provide a solution and you want to help them to ask them to buy your product or service that you are offering with a reasonable price. Right. So how to set out a pricing or how to actually sell your product or how to design your product is another topic that we cover. You may refer to my other cause.

I talk about how you can design a product, how you can start to drop shipping stores for physical products or how you can actually sell a digital product and start your own business. I talk about a lot of Borsos. Right. But the thing is, before you even have a product, after you have a product or after you have a pricing strategy on your mind that you want to set this price and. Right. The biggest problem to most people, especially, is those people who work in the big corporations as a stable job or, you know, doing their own thing without knowing a lot of people or some people who are very do not want to see people or meet people or do not have a lot of social connections. Right.

The biggest problem is how you can actually get to more people, acquire more customers. It's all about social networking. We're not talking about social networking websites that you're seeing on Facebook. Just that might be a tool you can use. But in concept, it's all about how you can get to know more people. And most importantly, those are highly targeted. The people who are interested in your product or who are working or in need, who can help you to get rich, who can buy a product, who can recognize your value, who can take your offer.

Those are the people you want to get to know and how you can get it right. That's the biggest problem for most people in this scenario. If you start a business already or if you know a lot of people already, you have a lease already. Right. That probably would be easy for you because you are starting to think the least. You give them some offer and let them ask them. See if this is a product created. Would you be interested to buy it? Right.

That's the thing you do. But if you do not have those, at least you can never run an Internet business before. How can you get it? It's all about getting popular, you know, to get those at or your potential customers the way you can get popular and get all the people to know you and your product. Right. In real, real words, not just talk about business in a relationship, a personal relationship or to other people.

You are talking about the people who give away a lot of freebies, get the most popular. Right, because you're creating more value. Right. Not necessarily free, but if you give a lot of other things to the people as they enjoy and you get a popularity and you get the customers right, singing about those are superstars like sports or entertainment. Right. They write their music that is so good and they share it with the world and people love it. And people want to buy all those sports stars. They play certain kinds of sports so well that they attract a lot of people who want to see them play and pay to see them play. Right. Same thing. Apply to your business. Right.

If your business, when they are starting out, will offer you, you do not have to offer your product for free constantly, but at least at the very beginning, you want to give away some free things to people. Right. Let them know you want them to come to your workplace, come to your store and to see you and know you and recognize their product. That's why when you start you can do all kinds of promotions, but it's either a or the same thing that you want to cut a price.

You want to get people to know you, or you want to put your product on the highest traffic of sites to get people to see your product. Right. And if people really see you either in the high traffic area or through paid advertising and they take your free offer to try a product knowing you and recognize a value, the problem will be more interesting to buy more products from you. That's the time. And you can be right.

Start your business. And that's the point. That's the point you want to go to. Right. But before that, you have to constantly be free content, free value to your customer. And you want to go to the most traffic sites to see all the people who give your product to them, madam, to see it. Or you can hire some promoters to promote your product or use unpaid social network advertising to promote your product. And either you want to let people see your product, you want people to like your product. And when some of the people, it's like a filter.

A funnel is all about filtering right to people. If they take your product right and the like, say, if all the people see your product, only maybe 200 of them like your product and want to know more. And then some people will get to the website and even try to protect that part of it down to maybe 15 or 20. Right. And among the 20s, maybe 10 of them buy a product. We're talking about a one percent conversion rate. Right. That's very good.

Not very good, but is a good sign that you're running an ad for yourself and the next thing you want to do is just repeat this process to expose your product to more people, to get more people, to see your product and the wisdom of people to buy a product. Right. But before that, you have to join. Read the least, generate the attention of your own people. That's where we're talk about lead a generation is so important because even though if you get to connect with people either through the email address or through some social network of followers, you get to know those of people you can contact with them, even not the they're not into the buying decision right away.

But you can contact them later on.

You can keep contacting us and letting them know that you're offering something right. So it's not about one time seeing that you kind of rush to make some money fast or really not. It's about constantly offering free values and giving away free things to your audience and letting them know you have something to offer. Let them know that you are so good with something and let them know that you can actually create some value for them.

And through the time as a young girl, there is a reason you can start to ask some wisdom into the buying decision. But if you don't have this relationship with the connection with them and they didn't even see your product is now never going to work. Right. So you will have to start over to focus on the lead generation as a lot of material we talk about in disBook to help you succeed.

I wish you the success of your business and the period here. And I want to see you in the next Book. Thank you.

Digital Marketing Strategy Profitable Sales Funnel Mastery

You might be surprised to learn that there are really only three ways to use digital marketing strategies to grow your business:

1. Increase the number of customers
2. Increase the average transaction value per customer
3. Increase the number of transactions per customer

And in this Book, you're going to learn how to execute on each one of these.

We will go through all of the ins and outs of creating profitable sales funnels that can help scale your business on autopilot while also giving your target audience an authentic and personalized experience throughout.

But I've often found that people don't end up succeeding with their sales funnel because they're trying to do too much too fast.

So in this Book, I want to overcome this problem by presenting the lessons in the following chapters, slowly increasing the level of difficulty.

Some marketers (including me) have been through years of trial and error to master the elements you will be able to master in just a few short hours in this class.

Are you ready to learn the exact sales and marketing strategies used by some of the biggest brands in the world?

I can't wait to see you on the inside!

Introduction

Have you been wondering exactly how so many successful marketers are able to create incredibly profitable sales funnels that generate thousands of dollars with every launch? The reality is, if you want to maximize your income so you can squeeze every possible dollar from your product launches, you absolutely need to master the art of creating high converting sales funnels.

And here's a fun fact: either you may think disBook was created to provide you with a step by step Quixtar blueprint to creating outstanding sales funnels to not only maximize your profits, but aimed at keeping the money rolling in long after your initial launch phrase is over. Before a while, castrati, the sales funnel that is based on proven techniques can take a single product launch and retain the momentum weeks, even months after the lunch.

Are you ready to learn insider strategies to turbo charge the sales funnels to maximize your income? If so, let's begin.

Overview of a Successful Funnel

Sales funnel mostly through a sales process and then make a final purchase, it introduces people to your brand who may not already be familiar with it, and it puts you in a position of connecting with our target audience.

It also amplifies a typical marketing strategy so that you are able to maximize profits and build your tribe and extend the life of product launch. The key is to create a sales funnel that makes sense to your target audience to overlook the importance of this, because not everyone in our industry responds the same way to a sales funnel.

It's not a one size fits all fits all approach. To begin, you will want to spend some time analyzing successful sales funnels in your market. Pay close attention to the price point that you're introducing along the way. What kind of cell do they offer? How do they move you from one offer to the next? Take notice of everything you need? You come across this information because this information will be helpful to you when you begin constructing your own funnel.

A sales funnel, which also helps to quantify traffic if it separates the action takers from the tire kickers, it works to create awareness of your brand and to test all different price strategies to find out a sweet spot. In other words, a search and Modibo purpose. Beyond the probability of the offer itself, your sales funnels objects to more traffic. And then came word that traffic along the way, you're inviting people into your funnel in order to connect with the potential customers and provide them with WERS options so that you are more likely to get the sales, even sales funnels that feature a single front end product designed to showcase other Erbakan offers throughout the process.

The one thing that many people overlook is that your funnel doesn't have to begin with a sale. In fact, you should look at the top of your funnel as an exploratory stage where customers are first introduced to your brand and are looking for reasons to buy from you. This means that your funnel may not begin on the sales page at all. It could start by following traffic into a mailing list in order to build your subscriber base and connect with your audience.

Your funnel may start with a blog that features high quality content and later encourages readers to become part of a Facebook group or a master class and newsletter. Or, Of course, it doesn't matter where or how your funnel begins. The important thing to keep in mind is that at the top of our funnel has one main goal to raise awareness of your brand and to connect with our potential customers and a funnel entry point or at the top of the funnel can be created in many ways, depending on your overall objective.

So to start thinking about what you hope to accomplish, do you want to be on the mailing list of people who are interested in your needs so that you can introduce them to new offers? Are you looking to start selling right away by creating a traditional sales funnel that begins with a low cost front end product? Do you want to get more important information from prospects that lead to Megaman free trials or free products before introducing them to pay to offers? Identify the main objective of the top of your sales, funnel first and then build your funnel around that.

The 3 Stages of a Successful Funnel

We were just discussing how the top injury, Epifano, doesn't always have the best selling effect. For many, this is the last place where they even consider doing a hard sell in. At the top of your sales funnel is an introduction phrase. As I have previously mentioned, it's where you allow people to get to know your brand. Kath's the waters and make the decision as to whether you have something valuable to offer. Here's how to create a top of your funnel stubley to capture a page. This can be a response to a page or a landing page.

The focus needs to be on capturing the lead of wire, a form that as a subscriber to your mailing list, you will want to offer something of a value exchange for your email address above different type of products featured within your funnel and offers on accountants the word of a product or something else that is relevant to your market outlook. The importance of the market.

If you want to maximize conversion rates, you will want to offer them something irresistible that instantly attracts attention from a free special report and the email based, Of course, for a series of chapters that you can get from Indigence or Stockholm. Always great ideas. The top of your funnel could be as simple as basic, a blog that provides killer content on your niche while directing people to another website where they can subscribe to a mailing list and download free content.

It depends on how you decided to try your funnel so that it maps out your marketing objectives. Once you have your injuries set up, it's time to move on to the castrato in the middle of your sales funnel. The middle of their funnel is where you begin the process of carefully collecting valuable information. It may also be where you start to convert that traffic into consumers through a series of lower costs of products and services.

This appropriate funnel is incredibly important because it's what helps you learn the most about your audience, such as what type of products and services they are most interested in. It can provide you with inside information we need to create on demand. The products were making it easier to cross-sell or up-sell to your customers related to products in your funnels. The Martok segment is where you may also begin to stop the sale.

Keep in mind that the goal is to strengthen your relationship with your audience as you guide them to the final stage of your funnel. The bottom line is the easiest way to create a powerful middle funnel is by offering valuable tools and resources for free. By combining those with a paid offer, Lembo used to offer a free five day email Book. Once they have graduated, you can introduce them to more in-depth pay to training that extends their knowledge on the topics or enhances the free material and the final at the bottom of your funnel.

This is a word you come by a balance of a hard and the softer sales, depending on how well you work the ad connecting to your audience. So all the top and the middle chapter of your funnel, you have a strong tribe by the time they reach this step.

Quick & Easy Funnel Research

If you are struggling to figure out what kind of sales funnel could work best for your business, you're few ways to gather important intel so that you can make the best. That decision. Social media channels spend time on social media, particularly paying close attention to existing sales funnels in your market.

Watch for comments, feedback and suggestions from customers. And consider creating a poll or survey for your own following so that you can gain valuable feedback

about what kind of product they are most interested in. Draw groups. You can also take things a step further by joining Facebook groups where you can interact with the people in your market.

In fact, you can always create a group of your own, which is a great way to get people into your funnel, white beauty or tribe or loyal customers. You can also drawn separated stress and a red is the separatist explorer influential bloc on the top 10 15 blocks in your niche and the follow the rest when you're looking for up laws that allow clickable signatures so that you can begin to generate the traffic to your funnel while also leaving comments that provide a valuable and relevant to each post.

Also, by spending time on sorority blocks, you'll stay up to date on discussions, keep a close pulse on your market and come up with new content ideas for your own website. And it's always a good thing to position yourself in the line of sight of an influential leader in your market, but also nurturing a relationship with their leaders. Readers. Google Trends A very effective strategy of funding.

Currently, Endemol is utilizing Google Trends. You can run searches based on poverty. Worse, identify you, find common searches and use this information as a basis for your marketing campaigns.

The Anatomy of a Profitable Sales Funnel

To begin to construct a successful sales funnel so you can begin to create your own a star with a front and often referred to as the FBI, offered to tripwire offer, depending on your goal or your former offer, could be a loss leader, meaning that price, the extremely low in order to get more people into the funnel was a loss leader.

As your front end product, you're not going to make the bulk of your profits from that initial offer, but rather different. Afsal offers features throughout a sales process. If you have never purchased a product through an online marketplace like GDL, chances are you have been introduced to a loss leader funnel. Perhaps you have purchased a front and offer at a price of ten dollars, only to be introduced to multiple offers.

Rather beckoned or priced at a higher than front, perhaps a funnel and move to something like this at the offer. Seventeen dollars for an e-book and the companion guys upswell offers No one seventy seven dollars for a series of meetings that serve as axillary components to the e-book. APSA offers to ninety seven access to a membership site that provides additional information and the new content every month now offering them online in that you learned someone didn't purchase a first Opsahl a little guy.

You could offer them a smaller collection of chapters at a lower price. This is a basic sales funnel and they can be as simple, as complicated and extensive as you wish. In the example above was a low cost upfront and offered you welcome people into your funnel by making it an easy decision to give your product a chance. Since there's a little risk on the customer's part, they're more likely to take advantage of the offer. But what if a customer who purchases your loan wants an offer?

Never purchasing any of your higher priced backend offers is still up with every customer that enters your funnel becomes a part of your base, broadening Minobe your tribe member, meaning they might not go to purchase regularly from you, but you're still able to make that connection to test the waters. A low cost front end sales funnel simply eliminates the usual barriers between your product and the customer who doesn't know your brand.

It puts you in a position where you can demonstrate your commitment to producing high quality products and potentially as a new member of your tribe. Of buyers, though jet fuel, a lower cost, the front and the sales funnel is simple. Get traffic and your subscriber base to convert that traffic into sales and segment your lease so that you are able to identify tribe members from those who are not likely to turn into loyal buyers. You can see an example of a typical sales funnel on the next page.

One of the most important things you can do to tighten up your middle funnel so you can maximize your profit is to consistently segment your lead. For example, you're going to have subscribers who are customers and subscribers for these leads that you haven't yet developed a relationship with. They might be interested in your offers and they haven't yet acted on it. Determine whether you exist only through your email communication with customers who have already purchased from you, already proven to be motivated active buyers.

Your relationship with these people is different from Leeth because you are able to establish a buying pattern and to demonstrate your ability to provide quality. They know what your product is like and what your style is, how you set yourself fondles around the most available subscriber you have. This is why it's critical that your segment, your segment on your list, you need to be able to communicate with the two groups separately with one you are working on conditioning them to purchase from you. Why?

With the other, you need to nurture a relationship to help get them to that stage in your funnel where they advocate auto service providers. The options to segment the person that you click funnel Stockholm to Bufano because they provide everything you ever need, including the testing options when they go well beyond. That was a funnel account. You can easily create automatic lead pages, landing pages and even membership sites.

Users spend most of their time testing your appearance so that you can maximize the number of subscribers while also being able to test the market's overall demand. It's a lot easier to convince someone to subscribe to your newsletter than to purchase a product. You'll be able to collect a lot more data based on action than even with their sales page. The more traffic you are able to send to your screens, the more subscribers you will get. So you need to make the beating a consistent part of your marketing campaign.

Split Testing Your Sales Funnel

You want to get into the habit of passing every aspect of your sales funnel speed, the testing is a way of passing specific elements on the sales page or within ourselves to improve conversion rates. The idea is to tax the one adamant at a time and run the passing campaign long enough to Bulls pages for both pages to generate a number of visitors. Here's an example of the basic Aspley testing campaign.

You create a tool sales page with two different highlights. You call them sales, page one in the cell. Page two uses and drives people to both pages equally so that both pages are receiving the same amount of traffic. Let it do its job for a reasonable amount of time. Usually seven to 10 days or into each page has received a spin specific, the number of visitors. The objective is to have a clear snapshot of which page is performing best based on conversion rates, eliminate the losers and the continual tweaking and testing.

Once you have established which page is outperforming the other, you change another element of the winning page and the comparative test against a different component. Another area of your sales pitch, such as your bullet points up in box placement or graphics Here's why speed testing is so important to you or to your sales funnel. Let's say your sales funnel is currently converting only one sale out of every one hundred visitors. And for this example, your product is priced at twenty dollars.

If only one visitor out of one hundred purchases your product, your conversion rate will be one percent. So you are simply testing your sales funnel. Perhaps you Yujin front and offer. So that is a slightly lower price and insulates your conversion rate increase by quarter one quarter percent, quarter of a one point one percent. Now you are generating five sales a day for every few hundred visitors to your site.

You are not earning one hundred dollars per day instead of 80, you continue to be the highest. Your sales funnel, the time to AFSA offer is priced slightly higher. This increases your conversion rate yet again this time is three quarters of one percent. Just a few small changes. You have boosted your conversion rate up by one percent and you now convert visitors out of every one hundred into a sale.

Your profit will have literally doubled over time. Sometimes even the smallest change in your funnel can cause a tremendous boost in revenue. And there was very little work involved. If you want to take the guesswork out of speed testing, take a look at a split. Having some monkey dot com on the part of software makes it easier to boost a sales increase option and then maximize your income with a little effort involved.

Final Words

Breaking a profitable sales funnel isn't as difficult as you may have seen the supply supplying every part of your funnel up front, that you can lay the groundwork for spewing a seamless system that moves traffic and commerce, feeds into buyers, and begins by deciding on where from and top will look like.

What ideas do you have that will influence a visitor into entering your funnel? You want to take advantage of a powerful lead to measurement that will motivate the business into subscribing to your mailing list, then singing about your funnel. What can they offer you? A that will help you further connect with your audience.

How can you demonstrate your commitment to fulfill your brand promise? And finally, how can you continue to provide a man who was starting to inform your audience about your core offer? Next, spend some time working on the bottom of your sales funnel. This is where you will make the most money. Consider different products and the services you offer them will appeal to your audience based on the intel you will get or that you need.

Funnel would and cross-sell will end whenever possible so that you are actively promoting the products that walk you to your audience. That is successful sales funnels from your competitors and always be on the lookout for ways you can expand your own funnel and above all else, stay consistent. You should focus on consistently improving your funnel by adding additional content that nurtures a relationship with your customer base.

Don't forget to engage leads in who may have reached the end of your funnel, but have failed to respond to your offers. A lot of traffic to increase your funnel. Maybe Kellert may not come to words, but if you spend time reconnecting with the audience, you're likely to win them over your success.

Conclusion

Hey, congratulations on finishing the sales funnel, cause this is a very important milestone, starting your online business and this business chapter, I want to share with you my personal experience. I started using the sales funnel. I know we have a cover, a lot of a series in this Quaritch.

What a sales funnel and why it's so important. And it was that basic element. Right. So let's do a case study on how I just actually did it. Right. So, first of all, I always think that when you actually start I come from a technology background. So when you actually see the online business, I kind of see it as a machine, that it's a machine that runs with the least effort. You know, you don't have to actually maintain it and naturally it can generate profit and cash flow for you.

I kind of think that in every machine there has to be a process, you know, to convert those inputs into output, hopefully some valuable output. Right. So definitely as a business, your goal is for the profit and also at the same time you want to provide value for your customer. So that's the output angle and input.

What it is, the input. You're actually reaching out to the people, right to the crowd, to the Internet. So that's why for any Internet marketing, you always go to the traffic sites nowadays, it's most likely the social networking sites. Right. So your input in the starting point is a social networking site of those biggest Internet traffic sites and they're who are actually getting some valuable value to your customers and also making some money, hopefully. Right.

So in between the inputs and outputs as well, we think of the sales funnel, it's like a building, a highway from point A to point B. Right. And in order to flow this whole data from point A to form B, you are actually making sure that No. One, the pipeline is Selt. The funnel itself is already a clean print. And that means that you do need to spend a lot of traffic there if you get lost somewhere in between. Right. And that would be a big problem. Right.

Another thing is that you want to make sure that you get the customer or the audience, your audience from the Internet, big sites. All right. Starting over eight points A actually can easily go to point B. Number one is that there's no such big traffic or connection that they are considering and don't understand where you are providing our offering. Right.

Number two is they can reach to the Gulf, to your goal to to Dirigo as well, because you have to have shared common values with easy or easy and also can gather some people when they actually travel from point A to point B, they have a different sort. They have the right to have questions as well. They don't know if they really want to get it or plan B, they don't know how to get A me. And last but not least, they are not sure about each step they are making. Right. Whether they should make it a step or two. Right.

So in typical Ansell's final week, the word is two different steps, right? You definitely do not belong to your audience to purchase, to create the purchase. Bonded right away because they don't have food. That is valuable information for them. Right. So you definitely want to offer something free. That's the fundamental law of the whole Internet marketing. That is, you don't just ask them for their purchase decisions.

You would definitely if you're a salesman, you go to a doctor. To a salesman. Right. You go to some house to sell, say, some household goods. Right. You don't just go in there and ask them, hey, buy this. This is a good buy. No, you want to demonstrate why this is good and how you can use it and you want to get to the same point whether their demand could be met with this product. That's how you are attributing the pipeline. So in each sales funnel, the first time will be you offering something to solve our problem or actually providing some values. Right.

You are asking them to actually get into ad free, to free freely, to try your product or your service they are providing. Right. So they get to the point where it's not typically if you want them to reserve this service. This is a trial for Distomo. Right. You want something to reserve this from this when you get to know who they are or what kind of work on the issue they have. Or what they would like to achieve.

It's like a straight basic A before you actually get your customer to trade them. Then you get to the demo day and in this demo party, you are actually just like a lifetime when you're giving a, you know, customer a demonstration that your product actually actively works right. To solve the problem. And you give some case study on how this will solve their problem as well. Right.

And you can even go to the scenario. You know, you assume you are him or her. Right. And then you can get their problem solved in the real world, they'll be more persuasive. And last but not least, when you actually do the demo and give all the information, give all the knowledge and share all the values, you can, you can generously ask them to, you know, consider the bias. Right. Because this is a value we are providing.

We're giving you the information or the service that you can try right. For free before you make the decision. And after all the work, after all the demonstration, Of course, you can definitely ask them to make the purchase decision. Right. So one way I do my own blog or beautify my honor and I promise is always giving out free either. Let's take an example of how I build my article. Right.

You attribute that to your posting content, but when you are posting content, either your content itself is entertainment, entertainment or very valuable information to share. You're always giving me something for free to your audience right in the same town in your chapter. You can't even offer some offline offers. If you asked, you asked them if I'm offering something for free to you in my chapter. You my profile. Right. So if they get your redial Tick-Tock recommended, I think you will get to show them.

First of all, the chapter itself has to draw their attention. A number two, by the end of your chapter, you always want to recommend them to go to your profiling, which leads them to your cell phone. And that's the starting point. And Salsano, its landing page and their landing pages. You actually see what they are actually offering. And they got an opportunity to try something for free and they can actually start there to actually experience the product you are actually offering. Right.

And then after they try their product and they experience that demo to actually return for more in-depth usage of your product and thus the time they actually make a purchase decision. That's how I formulated all my online products. Right. You don't want to get your customer to make the purchase decision right away. You want them to actually get into the room and get into the experience, you know, to use your product and most importantly, actually solve their problem if you can solve their problem and the knowledge alone.

So their problem, you can solve the problem and you can show them you can nicely solve the problem. Let them know if you can solve the problem. Your product is so good, but you don't have to process it. The sales fell on your top lawyer to lead them to actually experience that product. You would not be a success, right? But if you had a fantastic solution to solve the problem as well, you build a sales funnel to allow them to experience it and allow them to travel free until they made the decision to buy or not. Right. That's the point.

That's the whole point of how we actually want to run the Internet of business and definiteness else follow it not just by the funnel itself. That could be on the analytical part because you just step in this funnel nowadays with the technology and you can actually attach a lot of analytical tools. You can actually get to see where they click on the back page and the way how long they stayed on one page or one chapter and the wider hesitating user and clicking into your demo for free demo or click into the purchase decision.

That data can be collected by Google Analytics or Facebook page. So you can get to those data by making the analysis. Even if you consider only one customer that will be so. Right. But if you actually consider to actually run the data on Soldats of customers who visited your Web page, you can definitely find some pattern from here. And that's also important to make you actually get to know work to improve our sales funnel for the next iteration. Right. I hope you learn a lot from this Book.